DATE DUE

My   dier

JUL 06 2006			
AUG 05 2009			
JUL 20 2012			
FEB 21 2013			
GAYLORD			PRINTED IN U.S.A.

):

10 9 8 7 6 5 4 3 2

ISBN 1-889658-01-4

Second edition printed 2000. Printed in Korea

My daddy is a soldier.

Every morning he gets up really early to do "P.T." That means "physical training." Daddy says he has to exercise to stay in shape, and I help.

We do push-ups...

...and sit-ups.

Sometimes I ride my bike while daddy runs.

He irons his uniform every morning so it will be nice and neat. It is green and has lots of pockets.

He polishes his boots every day too. They are shiny and black, and a little too big for me...for now.

Sometimes daddy has to go to the field. It is kind of like camping, except Mommy and I don't get to go.

Daddy says he has to be ready for what-
ever job he might have to do. "Soldiers are busy
these days."

"They feed hungry people...

...they fight forest fires...

...they help people who have been in storms....

...and they take care of bad guys."

He packs up his tent, his sleeping bag, his extra clothes, and his canteen. He wears a big, hard hat, and he carries all of his things in duffel bags.

Daddy says when he goes to the field, it helps him to learn to be a better soldier, but I miss him when he's gone. I wish he had room enough for me.

Once daddy went away for a very long time. Mommy helped me write letters to him, and I drew pictures so he could hang them up in his tent.

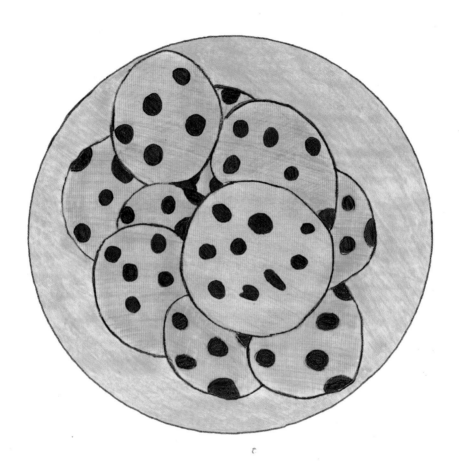

We baked cookies to send in daddy's care pack-
ages. Chocolate chip are his favorite. Mine too.

While he was gone, daddy wrote to me. I
checked the mailbox every day.

When a letter came, mommy read it out
loud. Daddy always said he missed us.

When daddy finally came home, he gave us lots of hugs and kisses.

He was really dirty, but mommy didn't make *him* take a bath.

One day, daddy said we had to move. Some people came to our house and packed all of our things into boxes and then put them into a big, yellow truck.

I was afraid they would pack Oscar, my turtle, but mommy said not to worry.

I had to say goodbye to all of my friends.

It was a sad day.

When we got to our new house, I saw some kids playing next door.

I went over and said "hi", and told them my name. They asked me if I wanted to play with them. Soon we were friends, and I didn't feel so sad anymore.

Michael said his dad is a mechanic, and he fixes big trucks.

Christina said her dad is a doctor, and he fixes people.

Tyler said his dad is a pilot, and he flies fast planes.

Ashley said her dad is a builder who makes giant skyscrapers.

And I said, "My daddy is a soldier."

"He helps make the world a safe place to live."